THE
COPPER
LADY

THE
COPPER
LADY

by Alice Ross and Kent Ross

illustrations by Leslie Bowman

M Millbrook Press/Minneapolis

Editor's note: The Statue of Liberty today looks quite
different from how it would have looked to André. The
statue's copper skin has become coated with a blue-green
film that protects it.

Text copyright © 1997 by Alice Ross and Kent Ross
Illustrations copyright © 1997 by Leslie Bowman

This book is available in two editions:
Library binding by Millbrook Press,
  a division of Lerner Publishing Group, Inc.
Soft cover by First Avenue Editions,
  an imprint of Lerner Publishing Group, Inc.
241 First Avenue North
Minneapolis, MN 55401 U.S.A.

Website address: www.lernerbooks.com

Library of Congress Cataloging-in-Publication Data

Ross, Alice.
   The copper lady / by Alice Ross and Kent Ross ; illustrations by
Leslie Bowman.
     p. cm. — (Carolrhoda on my own books)
     Summary: After helping Monsieur Bartholdi to build the Statue of
Liberty, a Parisian orphan stows away on the ship carrying the
statue to America.
   ISBN-13: 978-0-87614-934-8 (lib. bdg. : alk. paper)
   ISBN-10: 0-87614-934-4 (lib. bdg. : alk. paper)
   ISBN-13: 978-0-87614-960-7 (pbk. : alk. paper)
   ISBN-10: 0-87614-960-3 (pbk. : alk. paper)
   1. Statue of Liberty (New York, N.Y.)—Juvenile fiction.
[1. Statue of Liberty (New York, N.Y.)—Fiction. 2. Orphans—
Fiction. 3. Stowaways—Fiction.] I. Ross, Kent. II. Bowman,
Leslie W., ill. III. Title. IV. Series.
PZ7.R719615Co   1997
[E]—dc20   95–7628

Manufactured in the United States of America
9 10 11 12 13 14 – JR – 12 11 10 09 08 07

Authors' Note

The Statue of Liberty stands on Liberty Island in New York Harbor. The people of France gave this 151-foot-tall copper lady to the people of the United States in 1884. She is known around the world as an important symbol of the United States and of liberty, or freedom.

The idea for the statue began at a dinner party in France in 1865. The people there admired the United States. They wanted to create something that would celebrate the love of liberty shared by the two countries.

One of the men at the dinner was a sculptor named Frédéric Auguste Bartholdi (bar-TOHL-dee). The idea thrilled him. Right away, he started drawing sketches of a huge statue of a woman holding a torch. Over the next ten years, he made plans and raised money. Then he oversaw the building of the great lady.

When workers finished the shining copper statue, she was taken apart and put on a ship for her journey across the Atlantic Ocean to New York. Two weeks into the trip, a fierce storm arose, placing the ship and the statue in great danger. *The Copper Lady* is a fictional story about what could have happened during that storm. It is also the story of a young boy in Paris seeking freedom.

Paris, France
Late 1883

"Boy!" Louis Malet shouted.
"Have you been to that statue again?"
André tried to answer,
"Yes, but I did my work . . . "
Malet grabbed André
by the arm and yelled,
"No supper for you
if I catch you sneaking off again!
Now get the donkey and
load that cart!"

André shoveled the heavy coal.
As he worked, he thought about
the beautiful copper lady.
He pictured her shining eyes
and the torch she held.
André's parents had died
two years before,
when André was nine years old.
A neighbor, Louis Malet,
had taken him in.

In return, André was supposed
to help Malet deliver coal.
Before long,
André was doing all the work.
Malet gave him scraps to eat
and a spot in the barn to sleep,
but no pay and little freedom.
Still, no matter what Malet did,
André would keep visiting the Lady.

The next day before his rounds,
André picked an apple.
He carried it in his pocket
to make Josephine the donkey
go faster.
Finally, he dumped
his last load of coal.

Then he hurried to the shop
where workers were making the statue.
She was a gift from the French people
to the American people.
Some called her
Liberty Enlightening the World,
or the Statue of Liberty, for short.
To André, she was "the Lady."

André stopped in the wide doorway.
He loved the smells
of sawdust and steam,
plaster and wood,
fire and iron.

Sometimes he helped the men.

Today, he pumped the squeaking bellows

for the iron-workers.

They were bending red-hot iron bars

to form the Lady's skeleton.

He also carried nails

for the carpenters.

They were building wooden frames

and molds for the copper.

13

Most of all, André loved
to watch the coppersmiths.
Ping! Pang! Pong! rang their hammers
as the men pounded sheets of copper.

14

They turned the copper into
folds of the Lady's robe
and her reddish-brown skin.
The coppersmiths made her come alive!

15

André felt a hand on his shoulder.
It was Frédéric Auguste Bartholdi,
the man in charge of the statue.
"Back again, I see," he said.
"Yes, sir," André answered.
"May I hammer today?"
"I can't pay another coppersmith,"
Bartholdi replied.
"I will work for free,"
André said, hoping for his chance.
"All right then, you may try,"
Bartholdi said.

André found part of a wooden mold,
a hammer, and a scrap of copper.
Watching the coppersmiths,
he began to carefully tap
the thin copper sheet into the mold.
"You have a good touch, André,"
Bartholdi said later.
"Tomorrow you can work on the Lady."

The next day,

André carried *two* apples.

Josephine moved as fast as she could.

Soon he was pounding copper again.

"She's almost ready to go to America,

isn't she?" André asked Bartholdi.

"Yes, but the Americans

still need money

to build the pedestal for her

to stand on," he said.

"How would you like to climb up

to the Lady's crown?"

Behind the shop,

Bartholdi unlocked a door that led

into the statue's head,

which was already finished.

André and Bartholdi climbed the steps

to her crown.

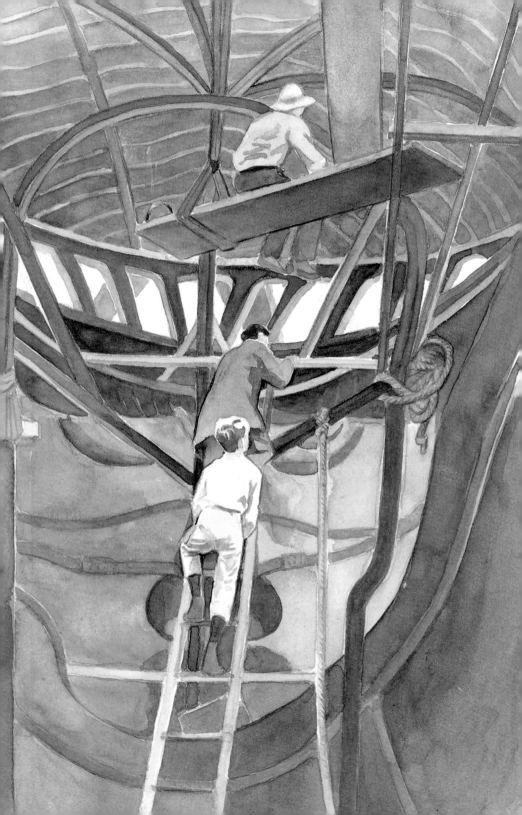

André boosted himself into
the crown's rim.
The workers below
looked like toy soldiers.
"Monsieur Bartholdi," André asked,
"why are we giving the Lady
to the Americans?
Couldn't we keep her?"

"She is a symbol of
friendship between France and
America," Bartholdi said.
"Both countries have fought
to gain the freedom for everyone
to live and work as they please.
The Lady will remind us all
to hold on to that freedom."

When they climbed down,
the sun was low in the sky.
It would soon be dark.
André hurried Josephine
through the streets,
but Malet was waiting.
"You're late again," he barked.
"No bread and cheese
for you tonight!"

As the days grew colder,
André worked longer hours,
often past dark.
He was sometimes hungry,
and his ragged coat could not
keep out the icy winds.

He made sure he came home on time,

but he visited the Lady often.

He helped beat the thin copper sheet

that became her little finger.

André laughed when he looked at it.

Her "little" finger

was seven feet long!

One day the next spring,

André stood beside Bartholdi.

They gazed up at the Lady.

She was finally complete.

From her torch to her toes,

she gleamed in the sun.

"Oh, Lady," André said,

"how beautiful you are."

A year passed before the Americans
finally sent for the Lady.
One morning,
André stopped Josephine
in front of the market.
A newsboy stood waving papers.

26

"Read about the Statue of Liberty!"
he shouted.
"What about her?" André asked.
"She's being taken down
to be shipped to America,
that's what," the boy answered.

27

That night in the barn,
André lay on his hard mat
thinking about the Lady.
He would never see her again.
He tried to imagine
what America was like.

He had heard stories
of how a young man could
earn a good wage and
make a new start there.
If only he could go with . . .
André sat up suddenly.
He had an idea.
It just might work.

May 20, 1885
Rouen, France

André hid behind a row of barrels.
Had the sailors seen him?
Back in Paris,
workers had taken the Lady apart
and put her in more than
two hundred wooden crates.

André had followed
the crates onto the train
to the ocean port.
Now the last crate was loaded
onto the warship *Isère*.
If he didn't get aboard soon,
the Lady would leave without him.

André took a deep breath.

Then he sprang into a hard run

up the gangplank.

Crouching behind a pile of rope,

he waited, listening.

His heart beat wildly.

From behind him,

André heard voices.

Two men walked closer.
André held his breath and tried
to sink into the shadows.
The men passed by without seeing him.
Now he had to find
a good hiding place.
Looking around, André saw a ladder
that led below deck.
He crawled to it and climbed down.

Now he was in the ship's hold,
where the cargo was stored.
In the dim light,
he could barely see the crates.
They had been tied to the sides
of the ship.
Quietly, he settled between
two of them.
As the ship jerked into motion,
André whispered,
"We're off to America, Lady."

For two weeks, André rode silently
in the gently rocking hold.
At night, he slipped above deck
to the ship's kitchen
for water and scraps of food.

35

One night, as he was returning
to the hold,
André heard boards creaking
behind him.
Someone was following him!
He could hear sailors mumbling.
"There must be a thief here
somewhere," one of them said.

Suddenly, the door to the hold
crashed open with a bang.
The ship heaved and rolled.
Wind whistled.
"Up deck! Storm coming!"
the sailors cried as they
stumbled up the ladder.
André breathed easier.

But then the ship began
to rise and dip,
higher and higher each time.
Crates strained against ropes,
groaning and whining.
Cold seawater dripped
onto André's neck.
All at once, the ship flew up
like a wild horse.
André tumbled across the hold.

He pulled himself up.

CRACK! SNAP!

One of the ropes was breaking!

With the next roll of the ship,

that crate would slide

into the others.

The Lady might be damaged.

André grabbed at the rope,

trying to retie it.

But it was stretched too tight.

He started for the ladder,
then stopped.
He knew that terrible things
happened to stowaways
who were found out.
He might be sent to prison,
or worse, sent back to Malet.

The ship tilted again,
higher and higher.
The loose crate shifted and bumped
against two other crates.
One of its boards split.
This time André climbed the ladder.
The Lady was more important
than his freedom.

Up on deck,

roaring waves blasted the ship.

Rain stung André's face.

He stumbled toward a sailor.

"Below!" he called into the wind.

"A rope has broken in the hold."

The sailor shouted orders.

Whistles sounded.

Two sailors followed André below.

With strong, quick fingers,

they tied up the loose crates.

The Lady was safe.

When the storm ended,
André was taken to the captain.
"So this is our stowaway,"
the captain said.
"You will work as a cabin boy
and then return to France."
André's face fell as the sailors
led him toward the door.
Suddenly, he shook free and cried,
"Wait, sir!
I only wanted to go to America
with the statue.
And I told about the loose crates."

The captain asked,

"What about your parents?"

"I have no parents," André said.

"And my master was cruel.

But Bartholdi let me work on the Lady.

I hammered copper for her hand.

I will earn my living in America

as a coppersmith."

The captain was listening now,
and André told him about the statue.
He described her flowing robes,
her crown, and her torch.
"She stands for freedom, sir,"
André said.
"Freedom for people to live
as they wish."

The captain thought for a moment.
Then he turned
to the sailors and said,
"Get this boy a mop and a bucket.
He may be a coppersmith in America,
but for now he is a cabin boy."
Hope filled André's heart.
He would stay with the Lady
in America.
With a smile on his face,
André headed for the deck.

Afterword

The Lady arrived safely in New York Harbor on June 17, 1885. During the next year, American workers finished the pedestal. Finally, on October 28, 1886, the Statue of Liberty was unveiled. A huge celebration took place. Boats filled the harbor, the president gave a speech, and New York City hosted a grand parade.

Over the years, immigrants to the United States have given the Statue of Liberty special meaning. Many immigrants remember her as the first thing they saw as they entered America.

Standing tall with torch raised high, the Lady seems to be welcoming immigrants and lighting their way to freedom. For all Americans, she remains a great symbol of friendship, liberty, and hope.